3/12/14

Why did
THE VIETNAM WAR
happen?

C<small>LIVE</small> G<small>IFFORD</small>

Gareth Stevens
Publishing

Please visit our Web site, www.garethstevens.com.
For a free color catalog of all our high-quality books,
call toll free 1-800-542-2595 or fax 1-877-542-2596.

Library of Congress Cataloging-in-Publication Data

Gifford, Clive.
  Why did the Vietnam War happen? / Clive Gifford.
      p. cm. -- (Moments in history)
  Includes index.
  ISBN 978-1-4339-4178-8 (library binding)
  ISBN 978-1-4339-4179-5 (pbk.)
  ISBN 978-1-4339-4180-1 (6-pack)
  1. Vietnam War, 1961-1975--Juvenile literature.
I. Title.
  DS557.7.G537 2011
  959.704'3--dc22
                          2010015835

First Edition

Published in 2011 by
Gareth Stevens Publishing
111 East 14th Street, Suite 349
New York, NY 10003

Copyright © 2011 Arcturus Publishing

Series concept: Alex Woolf
Editor: Philip de Ste. Croix
Designer: Andrew Easton
Picture researcher: Thomas Mitchell
Project manager: Joe Harris

Photo credits: All the photographs in this book were
supplied by Getty Images and are reproduced here
with their permission, except for cover image: Wally
McNamee/CORBIS, and pages 18 and 19: Bettman/
CORBIS. The photographs appearing on the pages
listed below are Time Life images. Time Life Pictures/
Getty Images: 28, 30.

Printed in the United States of America

CPSIA compliance information: Batch #AS10GS: For further information contact
Gareth Stevens, New York, New York at 1-800-542-2595.

SL001516US

CONTENTS

CHAPTER 1

A DIVIDED COUNTRY

Today, Vietnam is a southeast Asian country with a population of around 85 million people. China lies to its north, and Cambodia and Laos are neighbors along its western borders. However, for a period of more than two decades between 1954 and 1976, Vietnam was not one country but two.

The Vietnam War was an armed struggle in which South Vietnam, the United States, and its allies fought to prevent the Communists of North Vietnam from uniting North and South Vietnam under a Communist government. It lasted from the 1950s until 1975. While it was a military conflict, the civilian populations of both North and South Vietnam also suffered severely during the fighting. Over 2 million civilians and military personnel lost their lives during the war.

ASIAN EMPIRES

Vietnam was part of the French empire over a thirty-year period beginning in the late 1850s. Together with Cambodia and Laos, it was known as French Indochina. The British had established colonies in Burma (now Myanmar) and Malaya, the Dutch and British controlled what we now call Indonesia, and in 1898 the United States defeated the Spanish to establish a military presence in the Philippines. The colonial powers were attracted by the trading potential and the rich natural resources including spices, metals, sugar, rubber, coal, and rice. Under French rule, such commodities were shipped out of Vietnam without any benefit passing to the local people. A very few Vietnamese became wealthy by working with the French, but the vast majority gained nothing. Food was scarce for them while taxes were high. Some Vietnamese turned to their local governments for help, but these authorities were

Ho Chi Minh c.1940. He was one of the foremost leaders of the anticolonial movements in Southeast Asia, and helped form the Viet Minh to fight Japanese and French occupation of his homeland. He defiantly told the French in the late 1940s, "You can kill ten of my men for every one I kill of yours. But even at those odds, you will lose and I will win."

VOICES FROM HISTORY

Ho Chi Minh

Born in 1890 in North Vietnam, Ho Chi Minh left his country in 1911 to work as a kitchen hand on a French passenger liner. He traveled extensively in Europe and Asia and also visited the United States. He became a Communist in 1920 and a founding member of the French Communist Party. He was a passionate advocate of Vietnamese independence. His twin aims were to build an independent Vietnam free of foreign control and a nation ruled as a Communist society. In his declaration of independence for Vietnam in 1945, he stated:

"For more than eighty years, the French imperialists, abusing the standard of Liberty, Equality, and Fraternity, have violated our Fatherland and oppressed our fellow-citizens. . . . The entire Vietnamese people are determined to sacrifice their lives and property, in order to safeguard their independence and freedom."

Ho Chi Minh, *Selected Works Volume 3* (Hanoi, 1960–1962)

Japan on the move: trucks transport Japanese soldiers deeper into French Indochina during World War II. Indochina was occupied by around 30,000 Japanese troops during the war.

group of Communists whose burning desire was to achieve Vietnamese independence. Their leaders were Ho Chi Minh and Vo Nguyen Giap. In 1941, they formed the Viet Nam Doc Lap Dong Minh Hoi—the League for the Independence of Vietnam—better known as the Viet Minh.

At around this time, World War II (1939–1945) broke out in Europe. France was defeated by Germany and thus was powerless to defend its colonies in Asia. Japan invaded French Indochina, and by July 1941 had forced the French to let them run the colony. The Japanese stripped Vietnam of resources, and as a consequence hundreds of thousands of Vietnamese starved to death. Any protests against Japanese rule were dealt with harshly. But the Viet Minh grew stronger, and by 1944 was able to launch resistance attacks on Japanese outposts in northern Vietnam. By the beginning of 1945, the Viet Minh forces, commanded by Giap, had grown to over 5,000 and controlled parts of northern Vietnam.

powerless to change things, as they had no real political influence or significant money.

An undercurrent of opposition to French rule began to make itself felt in Vietnam. During the 1920s and 1930s, the French authorities cracked down ruthlessly on any hint of local unrest. Some rebels decided to band together in secret, and these movements gradually grew in strength. Among them were a

Three French air force fighter bombers on their way to attack Viet Minh ground forces at Dien Bien Phu in 1954. The French positions were besieged by the Viet Minh, and the French troops were eventually forced to surrender when the camp could no longer be supplied by air.

FRANCE TRIES TO REGAIN CONTROL

World War II ended in August 1945 when Japan surrendered after atomic bombs had been dropped on the cities of Hiroshima and Nagasaki. Japanese forces had to leave Vietnam, and the French authorities made plans to reassert their control in the region. However, the Viet Minh spotted their opportunity and acted quickly. In September 1945, they swept through the country's two largest cities, Hanoi in the north and Saigon in the south. In the north, the emperor, Bao Dai, was overthrown, and Ho declared an independent Vietnam. Ho Chi Minh hoped that the world would accept his country's independence from French

rule, but within three months, 50,000 French troops were back in the region. Four years later, Bao Dai was plucked from exile in Hong Kong by the French and installed as Vietnam's leader, but under their control.

During the First Indochina War, between 1946 and 1954, French and Viet Minh forces engaged in sporadic fighting. Giap was an astute military leader. He realized that guerrilla warfare tactics offered the best way to attack French forces. Familiarity with the local landscape meant that his men could mount a rapid attack and then melt back into dense tropical jungle. The Viet Minh's prospects improved enormously when China became a Communist country under the leadership of Mao Zedong in 1949. The Communist government of China was sympathetic to the Communists in Vietnam and supplied them with modern weapons and other equipment. As a result of this new source of munitions, the Viet Minh could step up the frequency and ferocity of their attacks. However, whenever they did engage in a conventional battle, they were badly defeated by superior French weapons. In a battle fought just 31 miles (50 km) north of Hanoi in January 1951, for example, out of a total force of 20,000 Viet Minh, casualties numbered 14,000 injured or killed.

The Viet Minh forces also worked hard to win the hearts and minds of the ordinary population. Viet Minh soldiers

French troops at Dien Bien Phu came under prolonged artillery attack by the Viet Minh. They established defensive positions in trenches.

Defeat at Dien Bien Phu

The defensive complex at Dien Bien Phu was designed to prevent Viet Minh forces from using a key supply route between Laos and South Vietnam. It was built in November 1953, close to the border with Laos. The French also hoped that their presence there might lure the Viet Minh into a large-scale battle—the sort of conventional military engagement that they were most confident of winning. However, Dien Bien Phu was situated in a valley, and the Viet Minh forces took up positions in the hills and surrounded the camp. They hauled Chinese-made antiaircraft guns and heavy artillery up mountainsides to bombard the French below. For 55 days, beginning on March 11, 1954, over 40,000 Viet Minh troops laid siege to Dien Bien Phu. The flow of supplies and reinforcements by air was also cut off when the airstrip was put out of action by heavy shelling. By early May, the French forces had suffered an estimated 7,000 casualties. On May 7, the French surrendered, and on the following day the French government announced its intention of withdrawing from Vietnam.

understood that they must be polite and fair, return borrowed property, and not steal or bully. Support for the Viet Minh grew as a result, especially in northern Vietnam, and new recruits flocked to their ranks.

A FULL-SCALE BATTLE

In an effort to stem the tide that was turning in favor of the Viet Minh, in 1953, General Henri Navarre, commander of the French forces, chose the site of Dien Bien Phu in the north of the country for a large-scale pitched battle with the Viet Minh. However, his tactics proved disastrous, and the Viet Minh besieged his positions and won. During the siege, the French turned to the United States for military assistance, but American leaders would not commit to military action

without the support of other allies. However, a peace conference had already been announced for the spring of 1954. Britain's declared policy was to pursue a negotiated settlement rather than risk military action. Other nations were also reluctant to commit troops on the ground, especially as the peace conference was already scheduled to be held in the Swiss city of Geneva.

In 1954, Vietnam was divided at the 17th parallel as a result of the Geneva Peace Conference. This created two states: the Democratic Republic of Vietnam in the north and the Republic of Vietnam in the south. Between them stood a demilitarized zone (DMZ) some 6 miles (10 km) wide.

A meeting underway at the Geneva Conference, held from April 26 to July 21, 1954. The conference resulted in the division of Vietnam.

Representatives from France, Britain, the United States, China, the Soviet Union, and the three French Indochina nations—Vietnam, Cambodia, and Laos—met in Geneva. The conference resulted in the publication of a series of documents known as the Geneva Accords. Cambodia and Laos were granted their independence with the promise of free elections to be held in 1955. Vietnam proved a harder problem to solve. The country was to be temporarily split between north and south along the line of geographical latitude known as the 17th parallel. The Viet Minh would withdraw to the northern portion—North Vietnam—under a Communist government led by Ho Chi Minh, while the French would pull back to non-Communist South Vietnam. An election for reunifying the two halves was to be held in 1956.

WHY DID IT HAPPEN

Did Vietnam have to be split in two?

Some historians argue that the division of Vietnam into two halves made further conflict inevitable. Others disagree, maintaining that granting Vietnam independence as a single country ruled by either a Communist regime or a non-Communist government allied to the United States would have increased tensions between the superpowers. Andrew Wiest writes that "In the end the superpowers did not want to risk global war over Vietnam" and dividing the country was the only way, at the time, that leaders felt this could be avoided.

Andrew Wiest, *The Vietnam War: 1956–1975* (Osprey, 2002)

CHAPTER 2

THE UNITED STATES IS DRAWN IN

During the late 1940s and early 1950s, the Soviet Union and the United States had established themselves as the world's two most powerful nations. In fact, they wielded so much influence that a new term had been coined for them: the superpowers. Despite fighting alongside one another as allies against Germany and Japan during World War II, in the postwar years their ideological differences had given rise to an atmosphere of mutual suspicion, with each deeply distrusting the motives and intentions of the other.

National security was an issue of paramount importance to both superpowers, and they worked feverishly to gain the upper hand by designing, testing, and stockpiling weapons in increasingly large numbers. By the mid-1950s, both the United States and the Soviet Union were fully aware of the massive damage and destruction that their nuclear weapons could do. They wanted to avoid a direct confrontation, but also wanted to continue to exert their influence around the globe.

BUILDING ALLIANCES

Both sides sought to bring sympathetic countries under their wings. They formed military alliances with other

The telltale mushroom-shaped cloud from a U.S. atom bomb test climbs into the atmosphere high above a Pacific Ocean island test site in 1950.

countries, donating aid, equipment, and weapons to assist the governments of friendly nations. On the other side of the equation, they also tried to overthrow the governments of some countries that were unsympathetic toward them, and replace them with friendlier regimes. For example, the Soviets invaded Hungary in 1956, while the United States trained and supported rebels who invaded and toppled the government of Guatemala in 1954.

The doctrine of Communism was deeply distrusted in the United States, and leading politicians and military figures were openly hostile toward the Soviet Union's Communist political system, which they feared would threaten the American way of life. In an attempt to halt the spread of this ideology to other countries, a policy of containment was adopted. The plan was to strangle the spread of Communism without provoking direct military action against the Soviet Union, in the hope that the Communist regime there would eventually collapse.

The Korean War (1950–1953) shows

VOICES FROM HISTORY

Falling dominoes

U.S. president Dwight D. Eisenhower laid great stress on the "domino theory" to explain U.S. foreign policy in Vietnam. He argued that if South Vietnam fell to Communism, neighboring countries would quickly follow.

"You have a row of dominoes set up, you knock over the first one, and what will happen to the last one is the certainty that it will go over very quickly. So you could have a beginning of a disintegration that would have the most profound influences. . . . Asia, after all, has already lost some 450 million of its peoples to the Communist dictatorship, and we simply can't afford greater losses."

President Dwight D. Eisenhower— Presidential Press Conference, April 7, 1954. Quoted in Stanley Karnow, *Vietnam: A History* (Penguin, 1991)

The Soviet Union was prepared to act ruthlessly to assert its influence. Here, Soviet tanks surround the parliament building in Budapest on November 12, 1956.

After landing on the west coast of Korea at Inchon in September 1950, U.N. troops—many of them U.S. Marines—advance toward the Korean city of Seoul some 22 miles (35 km) away.

how this policy was put into practice. Korea was divided into two halves, North and South, in the aftermath of World War II. In an attempt to reunify the country, the Communist North, under leader Kim Il-Sung, invaded South Korea in 1950. The United Nations sent an international force dominated by Americans to support South Korea. Neighboring China supported and armed Communist North Korea. The war was ferocious and costly, with over 3 million deaths including some 37,000 Americans. It ended with a cease-fire in 1953, but Korea remains divided today.

A DIVIDING LINE IN VIETNAM

Like Korea, in 1954 Vietnam was temporarily split in two. This was a result of the 1954 Geneva Conference (see page 8), but the solution did not satisfy the delegates from North and South. Ho and the Viet Minh had hoped that they would take control of more of Vietnam and that the elections would be scheduled sooner than 1956. Ho was riding the crest of a wave of popularity and was a strong favorite to win a national election if it was held immediately. For their part, the South Vietnamese were unhappy with the division of their country and the loss of so much territory. A North Vietnam run by the Communist Viet Minh was a cause for deep concern. The United States saw losing North Vietnam to Communism as a major setback. It now feared for

South Vietnam and was determined to stop another domino in the chain from falling.

The United States threw its support behind an anti-Communist government in South Vietnam and worked to help it become stable and capable of defending itself. In July 1954, Ngo Dinh Diem was made Vietnamese prime minister by Bao Dai. Diem, fearful of the Communists in the North, had refused to accept the decisions of the Geneva Conference and sought American support for his position. Diem did not impress some members of the U.S. government, but nevertheless the United States was prepared to back his authority in South Vietnam. His fervent anti-Communism was an advantage, he was already in a position of power, and, in the words of Secretary of State John Foster Dulles,

1955, Hanoi, North Vietnam: Ho Chi Minh attends a rally for young supporters. His government had just embarked on major land reforms in North Vietnam.

In 1955, the South Vietnamese leader Ngo Dinh Diem contested an election with Bao Dai on the future direction of South Vietnam. The results were rigged and Ngo claimed he had won 98.2 percent of the popular vote. The obviously falsified voting results appalled many South Vietnamese.

"We have accepted him because we knew of no one better."

AN UNPOPULAR LEADER

Bao Dai stepped down as head of state of South Vietnam in October 1955 after losing an election to Ngo Dinh Diem. The election was blatantly corrupt: in some places, Diem claimed more votes than there were total voters registered. Under Diem's presidency, South Vietnam experienced major unrest. He appeared to be more interested in securing his own position as leader than helping his population. When Vietnam was divided in 1954, around 900,000 Vietnamese in the northern region, who were fearful of Communist rule, had moved to the south. Finding homes, land, and work for these people should have been a priority for the new government. President Eisenhower hoped that Diem would push through reforms to help the local peasants obtain their own land, which they could farm in order to enjoy a better standard of living. Diem ignored land reform and instead moved his own supporters into positions of power in local areas. Far from helping ordinary people, these officials often forced them to work for unscrupulous landowners and to pay very high rents.

Diem's regime targeted other groups as well. Viet Minh sympathizers were hunted down and either executed or sent to reeducation prison camps. Religious grievances were also apparent. Diem was a Catholic, but most Vietnamese people were Buddhist. Diem tended to appoint only Catholics to important positions of power, and the Buddhist majority in the country was angered by what they saw as Diem's anti-Buddhist religious prejudice.

Ho Chi Minh in the North was equally critical of Diem's regime. His anger deepened when it became clear in 1956 that Diem was going to ignore the Geneva Accords and refuse to participate in a free election to reunite all of Vietnam. Ho did not confine himself to critical speeches. He ensured that the North Vietnamese regular army, the NVA, was built up in strength and forged stronger alliances with China and the Soviet Union. In secret, North Vietnam also encouraged some of its Communist supporters, dubbed "Vietcong" by the United States, to travel down from North Vietnam and start to infiltrate the South.

THE HO CHI MINH TRAIL

The next stage of opposition to Diem involved attacks by North Vietnamese guerrillas and targeted assassination of members of Diem's government. Between 1959 and 1961, an average of 4,000 officials were killed by Vietcong forces each year. Also in 1959, the North Vietnamese started building the Ho Chi Minh Trail. This 12,400-mile (20,000-km) trail was a complex web of truck routes, footpaths, and river systems running south from North Vietnam along the South Vietnamese border with Laos and Cambodia. Almost the entire trail lay just within the borders of these neutral countries and was beyond the reach of the U.S. and South Vietnam forces. Supplies and

A peasant farmer and his children outside Cu Chi strategic hamlet in South Vietnam. The peasant population of South Vietnam hoped that the ending of French colonial rule would lead to a better and more prosperous life for them. Yet, under Diem, the fortunes of most ordinary South Vietnamese peasants did not improve.

extra manpower were sent to South Vietnamese Communists along this route as the Vietcong's guerrilla warfare intensified.

In December 1960, Southern Vietnamese Communists established the National Liberation Front (NLF), dedicated to overthrowing Diem and reuniting North and South Vietnam. It took its message to ordinary people in

Female South Vietnamese guards are put through their drills at a strategic hamlet in 1962. The Strategic Hamlet program aimed to isolate the local population from the influence of the Vietcong.

villages and towns and rapidly gained popularity. To counter its effects, in 1962, Diem started to move peasants away from areas of the country sympathetic to the NLF into new, fortified village complexes. Reluctant people were forced away from their own communities and sacred family burial grounds. This tactic was known as the Strategic Hamlets Program. It actually alienated many peasants and fanned the flames of support for the NLF.

GROWING U.S. INVOLVEMENT

John F. Kennedy had become U.S. president at the start of 1961. He had vowed during his campaign to be tough on Communism and he stepped up the levels of aid granted to South Vietnam. In December 1961, he announced that more U.S. advisers would be sent to the country. By the time the Strategic Hamlets Program got underway, over 12,000 U.S. military advisers were in South Vietnam. Two years earlier, the number had been just 700. Kennedy was reluctant to send U.S. combat troops openly to Vietnam, but he supported the strengthening of the South Vietnamese army—the Army of the Republic of Vietnam, or ARVN—so that South Vietnam could fight for itself.

The ARVN had received hundreds of millions of U.S. dollars to equip and train itself since Diem's election in 1955. By 1963, it had grown in number

"A bottomless military and political quagmire. . ."

On a visit to France in 1961, Kennedy met with French president Charles de Gaulle, who warned him of the dangers of sending U.S. combat troops into Vietnam:

"The more you become involved out there against communism, the more the communists will appear as the champions of national independence. . . . You will sink step by step into a bottomless military and political quagmire, however much you spend in men and money."

Quoted in Hugh Brogan, *Kennedy* (Longman, 1996)

to 170,000 men, but it was not an impressive force. Morale among the troops was low and their commanders often argued. Vietcong forces frequently outwitted them in surprise attacks or outfought them in pitched battles.

In January 1963, for example, over 2,000 ARVN soldiers backed by U.S. helicopters took on some 350 Vietcong guerrillas near the village of Ap Bac. Although heavily outnumbered, the Vietcong triumphed, shooting down five helicopters and only suffering a handful of casualties. In an interview in September 1963, Kennedy voiced his frustration with the South Vietnamese

Senator John F. Kennedy is showered in ticker tape by excited crowds during his campaign for the U.S. presidency in 1960.

forces: "We can help them, we can give them equipment, we can send our men . . . as advisers, but they have to win it—the people of Vietnam—against the Communists."

THE FALL OF DIEM

For many South Vietnamese, dissatisfaction with their own government was a more pressing concern than the fight against Communism. The growing unrest, in South Vietnam intensified when protests by Buddhists in 1963 led to the arrests of thousands of Buddhist monks. Many simply disappeared. The army shared the feeling of unrest, and

TURNING POINTS IN HISTORY

The Gulf of Tonkin incident

On August 2, 1964, the American destroyer USS *Maddox* was fired upon by North Vietnamese torpedo boats while in the Gulf of Tonkin. It was there to support secret U.S. intelligence-gathering missions. President Johnson warned North Vietnam that any further aggressive action would lead to "grave consequences." Two days later, it was reported that the *Maddox* had again been attacked, although this later turned out to have been a false alarm. Up to this point, U.S. military involvement in Vietnam had been largely restricted to financial aid and advice. That now changed. The U.S. Congress passed a resolution allowing the president to take "all necessary measures to repel attacks . . . and prevent further aggression." It also stated that the president should assist any friendly southeast Asian state by taking "all necessary steps, including the use of armed force . . . in defense of its freedom." Johnson immediately retaliated with air strikes over North Vietnam.

Buddhist monks at a rally against the religious policies of President Ngo Dinh Diem on August 18, 1963. Some monks took the extreme step of setting fire to themselves in protest.

The road to war

Was the Gulf of Tonkin incident just a convenient excuse for the U.S. government to pursue a policy of committing troops to Vietnam, which it had already decided on? Historian William Michael Hammond notes that "President Johnson's advisers were deeply concerned and during July 1964 began to draft a congressional resolution sanctioning American attacks on North Vietnam as a means of stemming the communist tide." This was before the Gulf of Tonkin incident had taken place. Others argue that Johnson was considering it, but had not made the decision to escalate the war and send in combat troops until the incident occurred. Vivienne Sanders writes that "While Johnson was trying to decide whether there had been a second attack, the press reported the supposed incident and Johnson felt trapped, fearing that if he did nothing, his opponent in the presidential election [in November 1964] would call him a coward."

Dr. William Michael Hammond (contributor), *The Vietnam War* (Salamander, 1987); Vivienne Sanders, *The USA and Vietnam* (Hodder & Stoughton, 2002)

Vice President Lyndon B. Johnson is sworn into the presidency on November 22, 1963, hours after the assassination of John F. Kennedy.

on November 1, 1963, a military coup overthrew and killed Diem. The U.S. government had received advance warning of the coup but did not intervene, hoping that a stronger South Vietnamese government might emerge. Later the same month, Kennedy was assassinated, and Lyndon Johnson was sworn in as his successor.

In 1964, the new U.S. president and his advisers had to face the prospect that South Vietnam would need far more military support to stop it from falling into Communist hands. Then, an incident in the Gulf of Tonkin (see opposite) gave Johnson the power to greatly increase the United States' military involvement in Vietnam.

CHAPTER 3

BATTLE IS JOINED

At first, the United States resisted the temptation of sending in large numbers of ground troops. Instead they launched air attacks, increased the numbers of military advisers in the country, and tried to bolster the strength of the ARVN. However, the ARVN's best troops suffered a series of damaging defeats in December 1964. Then, the Vietcong attacked U.S. barracks in Pleiku in February 1965, killing eight Americans and wounding more than one hundred. It was obvious that a change of tactics was needed.

A full-scale invasion of North Vietnam was not in the cards. Lessons had been learned from the Korean War and there were fears that China or the Soviet Union might retaliate by sending troops to defend North Vietnam. A huge bombing campaign of North Vietnam was chosen instead, in the belief that the U.S. Air Force could batter the North Vietnamese economy sufficiently to force North Vietnam to stop supporting the Communists in South Vietnam.

A U.S. McDonnell Douglas F-4C Phantom comes in low to drop bombs on a suspected Vietcong hideout. Hundreds of Phantoms saw service—some equipped as bombers or fighters, while others flew reconnaissance missions or were used to strike at enemy missile sites.

A long campaign: three years of bombing

U.S. military involvement in Vietnam increased significantly when Operation Rolling Thunder got underway in 1965. At first, the U.S. Air Force was confident that a huge series of bombing raids flown by the world's most powerful and best equipped air force would tip the balance in its favor. The raids were meant to make clear the U.S.'s determination to fight to the finish, as well as to destroy North Vietnam's industry and break the resistance of its people. However, North Vietnam was basically a peasant economy—it did not have many major industrial targets. Another factor was that some important targets, especially those close to the Chinese border, were avoided for fear of drawing China into the conflict. During the Rolling Thunder operation, over 1 million tons of bombs were dropped on North Vietnam. They caused great damage and much human suffering, but the bombing did not batter North Vietnam into submission or force its leaders into peace talks.

The first U.S. combat troops to be openly deployed to the war come ashore at Da Nang in March 1965. They were among the 3,500 U.S. Marines who formed the first detachment.

OPERATION ROLLING THUNDER

Regular, heavy bombing raids on North Vietnam and Communist strongholds in parts of South Vietnam began on March 2, 1965. The operation was code-named Rolling Thunder. Some of the aircraft flew from aircraft carriers in the South China Sea; others were deployed from air bases in South Vietnam or Thailand. The plan was to continue the bombing campaign for just eight weeks, but it actually stretched on for almost three and a half years, during which time over 1 million tons of bombs were dropped.

The next development was the arrival, also in March 1965, of the first publicly declared U.S. combat troops in South Vietnam, a detachment of some 3,500 marines. Rolling Thunder and the dispatch of troops were described to the American public as being short-term measures only, and public opinion in the United States was generally supportive. The bombing was halted briefly in May as the United States

The commander of the U.S. forces in Vietnam, General William Westmoreland, inspects the 1st Infantry Division in 1965. This unit lost more than 3,000 soldiers killed in action.

tried to open peace talks with North Vietnam, but this was unsuccessful. Another attempt was made in December 1965, but it again failed, and bombing resumed in February 1966.

Along with the military campaigns, both sides also launched a propaganda offensive. The United States claimed that it was helping a free nation defend itself from attack by a hostile neighbor. They and the South Vietnamese depicted the Communist NLF and Vietcong as being orchestrated by the North Vietnamese government. The North Vietnamese, for their part, characterized the conflict as a war between rebels who had the support of most South Vietnamese and a corrupt South Vietnam government that was

nothing more than a puppet of the United States.

The NLF responded to Operation Rolling Thunder by concentrating its attacks on U.S. military air bases in South Vietnam. General William C. Westmoreland, who had been the commander of U.S. forces in Vietnam since the middle of 1964, was concerned that he did not have enough soldiers under his command to defend the air bases from attack. More combat troops began to arrive in South Vietnam, and by the end of 1965, Westmoreland was leading an estimated 180,000-strong force. Soldiers from Australia, Thailand, New Zealand, the Philippines, and South Korea eventually joined the force. However, two of America's firmest Cold War allies, Canada and Britain, declined to send troops—although an estimated 30,000 Canadians did sign up to serve in the U.S. military during the war.

SEARCH AND DESTROY

Westmoreland was convinced that the best chance of success would come through adopting aggressive tactics, known as "search and destroy." U.S. forces actively sought out NVA units operating in South Vietnam and strongholds of the Vietcong. Once the enemy was located, the Americans would call in reinforcements. These included helicopters and aircraft carrying troops, heavy artillery, and squadrons of bomber aircraft.

The United States believed that its superiority in military technology would allow it to control the seas around Vietnam and the airspace above it. It bombed known Communist supply routes, among other targets, and sought to gain complete supremacy in the air. The latest weapons were used by its aircraft, including "smart" missiles that could be automatically locked onto their targets.

Battle tactics on the ground were based on trying to fight a conventional war; if the enemy could be drawn into major pitched battles, the U.S. military could employ its superior weaponry and would be more than a match for them. In November 1965, the first major ground battle involving U.S. troops appeared to prove this point. A short, fierce battle in Ia Drang Valley was resoundingly won by the Americans. However, actions like these were few and far between. The U.S. military found it difficult to uncover the Vietcong and NVA and to draw them into large-scale pitched battles. The Vietcong, in particular, proved very hard to pin down, as they were organized into small cells and tended to move and attack at night.

U.S. Army Air Cavalry disembark from Bell UH-1 Huey transport helicopters. A mainstay of the U.S. armed forces, the Huey was used mainly as a troop transporter or as a medical air ambulance. Over 2,500 Hueys were lost in Vietnam in operational accidents or through enemy fire.

TOTAL U.S. MILITARY PERSONNEL IN VIETNAM

DATE	TOTAL PERSONNEL
December 31, 1960	900
December 31, 1961	3,200
December 31, 1962	11,500
December 31, 1963	16,300
December 31, 1964	23,300
December 31, 1965	184,300
December 31, 1966	425,300
December 31, 1967	485,600
December 31, 1968	536,100
December 31, 1969	474,400
December 31, 1970	335,800
June 9, 1971	250,900

Source: www.globalsecurity.org

VOICES FROM HISTORY

Losing hearts and minds

Ordinary South Vietnamese villagers were often treated harshly by the ARVN or American forces, if any evidence of the Vietcong was found. By contrast, the Vietcong sought to win the support of the rural villagers. U.S. Marine William Ehrhart describes what might happen:

"They'd be beaten pretty badly, maybe tortured. Or they might be hauled off to jail, and God knows what happened to them. At the end of the day, the villagers would be turned loose. Their homes had been wrecked, their chickens killed, their rice confiscated—and if they weren't pro-Viet Cong before we got there, they sure as hell were by the time we left."

William D. Ehrhart, *Busted: A Vietnam Veteran* (University of Massachusetts Press, 1995)

GUERRILLA WARFARE

The Vietcong wanted to fight a guerrilla war using techniques that had been refined by many years of combat against the Japanese, French, and South Vietnamese. Their tactics were brilliantly suited to Vietnam's geography: it is a land of hills, forests, and large areas of boggy ground. Small groups of lightly armed men carrying rifles, machine guns, mortars, and grenades could move around freely, but large military vehicles, such as tanks, struggled to operate there. The Vietcong were able to attack and harass American and South Vietnamese targets and lay secret booby traps, taking advantage of their knowledge of the terrain. Some traps were pits filled with sharpened stakes concealed by a layer of twigs and leaves. Other traps triggered hidden explosive devices. After laying their booby traps, the Vietcong would melt away deep into the jungle or into secret hideouts, such as tunnels, or cover their tracks in rural villages that were sympathetic to them.

The Vietcong particularly wanted to win the support of ordinary villagers. Most peasants in the villages were poor, owned no land, and had to work for rich landowners. When the Vietcong took control of a village or area, they often dismissed or executed the landlords and divided the land among the peasants. Naturally, this made them popular with village people, some of whom they

The major engagements fought between 1965 and 1967 in South Vietnam extended from Khe Sanh in the north to the Mekong Delta in the south.

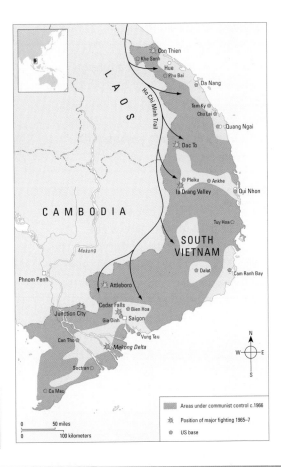

recruited to their cause. Villages that resisted or opposed the Communists, however, were often attacked and destroyed.

Another factor that worked in favor of the Vietcong was that they were used to the climate, conditions, and terrain found in Vietnam. Many of them had been using guerrilla tactics for many years, and they were a highly experienced fighting force. By contrast, the average age of the

American field guns pound a Vietcong position in April 1968. The Americans relied greatly on firepower both on the ground and in the air.

American soldier in Vietnam was just nineteen. For many of them, this was their first tour of duty in a foreign country. They were very inexperienced and felt uneasy having been plucked from the safety of the United States to fight a war in such an unfamiliar country.

A Problem of Morale

Another factor that put the American forces at a disadvantage was the shortness of the tours of duty that they made. Most of them lasted only one year. By the time soldiers had gained some valuable experience fighting in Vietnam, they were shipped home again to the United States. Inexperienced new arrivals in Vietnam were viewed with

A young U.S. soldier cradles his M16 rifle and looks out warily from a position deep in the Vietnamese jungle.

VOICES FROM HISTORY

"They all looked alike."

The constant fear of the next attack took its toll on young U.S. ground troops who often could not tell friend from foe. U.S. Marine captain E.J. Banks recalled:

"You never knew who was the enemy and who was your friend. They all looked alike. They all dressed alike. They were all Vietnamese. Some of them were Viet Cong. Here's a woman . . . she tells an interrogator that . . . she isn't Viet Cong. But she watches your men walk down a trail and get killed or wounded by a booby trap. She knows the booby trap is there, but she doesn't warn them. Maybe, she planted it herself."

Captain E. J. Banks quoted in Stanley Karnow, *Vietnam: A History* (Penguin, 1991)

mistrust by battle-hardened veterans. Consequently, the new men were often isolated or given the most dangerous tasks by more experienced soldiers.

The language, people, and surroundings were all totally unfamiliar to the Americans, some of whom had only just left school. They suffered from the intense heat and humidity and from mosquito bites and tropical diseases, such as malaria and dysentery. Many had little stomach for the fight and were in a state of almost constant anxiety caused by the Vietcong's style of guerrilla fighting. American soldiers were used to fighting wars in which it was easy to identify your enemy and bring him to battle. In Vietnam, they could not tell who was a friend

and who was a foe.

EBB AND FLOW

Throughout 1966 and 1967, more and more U.S. and allied troops were committed to this unfamiliar theater of war, but the type of warfare rarely changed. The Vietcong would engage in hit-and-run attacks. The Americans would respond with search-and-destroy missions. There were times when U.S. troops won significant victories in a particular area, but they were generally unable to take permanent control of the location.

One U.S. tactic that was adopted in rural regions was to eliminate hiding places by destroying the jungle cover and choke off supplies by targeting the routes along which arms and equipment were transported. Supply routes were bombed and U.S. aircraft flew missions to spray chemicals called defoliants on trees and bushes. These worked by killing their leaves and stripping them

Operation Cedar Falls: American forces direct flamethrowers at the trees and bushes around a Vietcong stronghold called the Iron Triangle just 31 miles (50 km) away from Saigon.

bare of foliage. U.S. forces bulldozed and destroyed networks of tunnels, tracts of forest, and even entire villages that were sympathetic to the Vietcong. Yet despite these tactics and the increasingly heavy losses that were inflicted on the Communists, the Vietcong and NVA always found ways of resupplying themselves with stores and weapons.

Some U.S. political and military leaders began to believe that the course of the war might be turning in their favor in 1967, as Vietcong and NVA losses mounted heavily. However, in the following year, the Tet Offensive signaled a major change in the fortunes of both sides. As a result of it, more and more American people, some of them in

27

In 1968, 6,000 U.S. soldiers at Khe Sanh held out during a 77-day siege of the American base there, with the assistance of heavy aerial bombardment from American aircraft and helicopter gunships. These U.S. Marines are waiting to move up to Khe Sanh as reinforcements.

positions of power, began to argue that the war was essentially unwinnable.

Khe Sanh and the Tet Offensive

The military situation on the ground changed radically at the start of 1968. The North Vietnamese leadership decided to go on the offensive. The campaign began with a massed attack on and siege of a 6,000-strong U.S. military base at Khe Sanh by NVA troops and Vietcong guerrillas. The base was an important position for the Americans, and the North Vietnamese hoped that this attack would act as a diversion to draw U.S. attention away from another sector where they intended to launch a major offensive. This was unleashed on Tet Nguyen Dan, the Lunar New Year (January 30–31, 1968), a traditional holiday in Vietnam.

The North Vietnamese completely changed their tactics. Giap felt that he should attempt to win a major, and possibly critical, victory by engaging the Americans in an open battle sprung with the element of surprise. Guerrilla tactics on this occasion would be set aside. The Communists also hoped that such a showdown with the United States would encourage large numbers of sympathizers in South Vietnam to rise up and join them. A series of attacks on 100 South Vietnamese towns and cities was launched by around 85,000 Vietcong and NVA. The Tet Offensive was relatively successful at first, as the Communists advanced into many major cities including Hue and Saigon. Because of the public holiday, more than 40 percent of the South Vietnamese army was absent on leave. In Hue, the NVA held on to their gains for over a month, during which

WHY DID IT HAPPEN

The wrong strategy?

Was the U.S. military trapped into fighting the wrong sort of war in Vietnam? Historian Douglas Pike asserts that "the American military's performance was particularly impressive. It won every significant battle fought, a record virtually unparalleled in the history of warfare."

Historian Andrew Krepinevich disagrees, and maintains that the United States was misguided in its conduct of the war. It did not do enough to deal with the political struggle waged by the Vietcong to win over South Vietnamese. It also failed to develop more flexible fighting skills such as "long-term patrolling of a small area, the pervasive use of night operations, emphasis on intelligence on the insurgents," instead opting for "conventional war and a reliance on high volumes of firepower."

Douglas Pike, *PAVN: People's Army of Vietnam* (Da Capo Press, 1991); Andrew Krepinevich, *The Army and Vietnam* (Johns Hopkins University Press, 1986)

they hunted down and killed between 3,000 and 6,000 South Vietnamese government supporters. Elsewhere, though, within one or two weeks fierce fighting drove the Communists back with huge losses. The siege of Khe Sanh lasted until April 8, when a U.S. relief force finally got through. In total, the Communists lost between 45,000 and 58,000 troops at Khe Sanh and during the Tet Offensive. Militarily, the offensive can be judged a failure for the Vietcong and NVA. However, it did bring home to senior U.S. politicians, generals, and the general public the fact that the war was far from being won.

A U.S. serviceman carries an M60 machine gun through the streets of Hue after American troops had cleared the NVA out of the city.

CHAPTER 4

VOICES OF PROTEST

The times were changing in 1968 in the United States. It was a year of protest and the antiwar movement was gathering strength. It had taken root as early as 1964–65, chiefly among college and university lecturers and students. Some were very critical of the support that the United States gave a brutal South Vietnamese government. Others were pacifists (i.e., against all wars).

Some were suspicious of economic motives, believing that the United States had gone to war principally so that it could take advantage of valuable raw materials in Vietnam and neighboring southeast Asian countries, and make a profit by selling them American-made goods.

However, most Americans still supported their president's actions in Vietnam and believed that the spread of Communism must be halted. The U.S. government was careful to depict the conflict as a limited, strictly defined action that would not be allowed to escalate into a war between the superpowers. Many U.S. citizens felt threatened by Communism and generally supported attempts to limit its influence in other countries. Public opinion remained convinced that the U.S. military would bring the conflict to an end, and Americans were proud of their country's leading role in the fight against Communism.

GROWING DISCONTENT

However, the lack of a rapid clear-cut victory began to feed antiwar sentiment in the United States. The casualty figures were mounting as more troops were sent to the combat zone. Between

Helicopter crewman James Farley calls for medical assistance for an injured pilot who was being evacuated in Farley's aircraft. The pilot, James Magel, died of his wounds.

1961 and 1965, the United States lost 1,864 personnel killed in action. In 1966 alone, it lost 6,000, and in 1967 over 11,000. More and more young Americans were drafted to serve in the war. For communities across the United States, this war was no longer a distant phenomenon—it had become uncomfortably personal.

Vietnam was the first war that was covered by television reporters virtually as it happened. Television beamed pictures from the frontline directly into the homes of people back in the United States in a way that had never happened before. News reports and TV footage revealed the casualties suffered not only by U.S. soldiers and their allies, but also by civilians caught up in the fighting throughout South Vietnam. Many viewers were horrified by the use of weapons such as napalm, a type of jellied gasoline that sticks to skin, flesh, and muscle as it burns. Opposition to the war began to mount. The human suffering in Vietnam was not the only controversial issue. Many people were deeply concerned about the rising cost

Televised reports from the frontline by journalists such as CBS TV news reporter Dan Rather graphically conveyed the brutality of the war to audiences watching at home in the United States. The Vietnam War was the first major conflict to be extensively televised.

VOICES FROM HISTORY

Homegrown critic

One of the few voices within Johnson's administration opposed to continuing the war was that of Undersecretary of State George Ball. In 1966, in memos to the president, he wrote:

"From our point of view, the terrain in South Viet-Nam could not be worse. Jungles and rice paddies are not designed for modern arms. . . . Politically, South Viet-Nam is a lost cause. The country is bled white from twenty years of war and the people are sick of it. . . . Hanoi has a Government and a purpose and a discipline. The 'government' in Saigon is a travesty. . . If ever there was an occasion for a tactical withdrawal, this is it."

U.S. Department of State S/S Files Lot 70 D 48

A huge fireball erupts as the U.S. Air Force tests a napalm bomb at Elgin Airfield in Florida. Napalm was a mixture of gasoline and a thickening agent. It could be propelled by flamethrowers or dropped as incendiary bombs. Once burning, it was very difficult to put out. It was used extensively in Vietnam.

of the war (believed to be as much as $20 billion in 1968, for example). Taxes were rising, and social services programs were being cut, as the war sucked money out of the economy.

Even people close to President Johnson began to express their doubts. Secretary of Defense Robert McNamara became increasingly skeptical about America's involvement in the war. McNamara was influenced by his son and daughter, who were both antiwar demonstrators, and by a nagging fear that his country could not win the war. In November 1967, McNamara resigned his position.

The public mood of doubt and disquiet deepened further when the Tet Offensive was launched in January 1968 and pictures of the savage fighting were broadcast on television screens around the world. U.S. military and political leaders had been trying to reassure the American public that the war would not last much longer. After Tet, increasing numbers of Americans doubted this to be true. While they may not have taken to the streets with the antiwar protesters, many ordinary Americans blamed their president for prolonging the war or for adopting the wrong strategy. Johnson's approval rating in opinion polls plummeted, and his health started to suffer. On March 31,

1968, he announced he would not run for re-election as president.

A NEW PRESIDENT

The Vietnam War was the burning issue that dominated the presidential election in November 1968. The victor, Republican Richard Nixon, promised during his election campaign that he would seek "peace with honor." The electorate was split down the middle. The growing antiwar movement was concerned by mounting casualties and wanted the United States to pull out. On the other hand, many Americans continued to support U.S. involvement in Vietnam. They believed that the United States was right to fight this war to prevent Communists from taking over a free country. Reports circulated

of Communist atrocities, especially the murders of civilians. It seemed clear that the Communists had to be stopped and that the South Vietnamese needed U.S. protection.

Then came a disturbing development: stories of atrocities committed by the United States' own soldiers reached the American public. News of the My Lai massacre broke in 1969 and the world was horrified. This incident gave rise to

In a highly symbolic gesture, antiwar protesters burn their draft cards during a 1967 demonstration in Washington, D.C. The draft was a system whereby young men were required by law to serve in the military. Some people believed that the draft was biased because fewer middle-class, wealthy Americans were drafted to serve in Vietnam than members of poorer ethnic minorities.

Massacre at My Lai

Americans were horrified when they received news in 1969 of a massacre of civilians by U.S. troops. In March 1968, U.S. soldiers led by Lieutenant William L. Calley Jr. burned down the village of My Lai and killed 357 women, children, and elderly men living there, as well as 150 more people in nearby hamlets. The army covered up the massacre. A year later, a soldier from another unit heard about the incident and contacted his congressman. *The New York Times* broke the story. The atrocities caused widespread public outrage and disgust.

The village of My Lai burns and a U.S. soldier fans the flames with a flat basket used to dry rice. My Lai was the scene of one of the worst atrocities committed by U.S. troops during the Vietnam War. When news of the killings emerged, world opinion was outraged.

a protest organization called Vietnam Veterans Against the War (VVAW). This group, which was founded in 1967, filmed about 100 veterans confessing that atrocities like those committed at My Lai, even if they were not on the same horrific scale, had happened at other times during the war.

VOICES RAISED IN PROTEST

Many other antiwar groups voiced their opposition to the fighting between 1967 and 1969. Protests and demonstrations became larger and more frequent. Coordinated National Moratorium antiwar demonstrations took place across the United States on October

15, 1969. Hundreds of thousands of people took part. Exactly a month later, a second round of demonstrations occurred. This time over a quarter of a million people took to the streets in Washington, D.C. People from all walks of life wanted to protest, and for many different reasons. Some were appalled at the human suffering or the financial cost of the war. Others feared that the war was simply not winnable, or could not understand why U.S. troops should fight a war on someone else's behalf. One thing was clear—the government could not ignore these voices raised in opposition to the war.

Antiwar feelings were not confined to left-wing radicals or confirmed pacifists. In 1971, a group of Vietnam War veterans camped in the National Mall park in Washington, D.C., for a week to protest the war. Fifty veterans tried to turn themselves in to the military authorities in the Pentagon as war criminals for taking part in a war that they felt was wrong and unlawful.

WHY DID IT HAPPEN ?

Why did public opinion turn against the war?

Many people blamed the media for turning the American public against the war. However, some historians, including William Hammond and Philip Taylor, have doubts about this. Hammond argues that military strategy in Vietnam and political decision-making back in Washington were far more responsible for swaying public opinion than negative media coverage. In fact, the Vietnam War continued for five years after the Tet Offensive and My Lai and enjoyed the support of many Americans during this time. This, Taylor reasons, must "raise some doubts as to the validity of the thesis that the Vietnam War was lost on the domestic front by a hostile media."

Marshall McLuhan, a famous Canadian media scholar and philosopher, disagrees. In 1975, he pointed out that "television brought the brutality of war into the comfort of the living room. Vietnam was lost in the living rooms of America—not on the battlefields of Vietnam."

Philip M. Taylor, *Munitions of the Mind,* *3rd Edition* (Manchester University Press, 2003); Marshall McLuhan, *Montreal Gazette* article, May 1975

CHAPTER 5

THE END OF THE VIETNAM WAR

U.S. forces in Vietnam reached their maximum levels of about 540,000 in 1969, Nixon's first year in office. From this time on, American troops would be gradually withdrawn. In June, Nixon announced the departure of 25,000 troops. Secret peace talks got underway in August 1969. Then another 65,000 troops were shipped back to the United States by the end of the year. Troop numbers dropped significantly in the next two years. By the end of 1971, American forces in Vietnam numbered 140,000.

However, although troop numbers were falling, U.S. casualties continued to mount and antiwar opposition got more intense. It was fueled by revelations of more atrocities and plummeting troop morale, which led to record numbers of desertions and attacks by soldiers on their own officers. In 1970, U.S. forces controversially invaded Cambodia to destroy Vietcong bases and supply routes in that country. This provoked more outrage from a world fearing a "second Vietnam." The invasion achieved little and the troops withdrew after two months.

VIETNAMIZATION

A new strategy was put into effect in 1971. Known as Vietnamization, it had been developed by Nixon and his secretary of state, Henry Kissinger. It was designed to create a strong, self-reliant South Vietnam powerful enough

In April 1970, President Nixon authorized a limited incursion into Cambodia to support the new regime of the pro-American leader, Lieutenant General Lon Nol. Here, a U.S. armored personnel carrier advances into Cambodia past the bodies of two local casualties.

Secret papers are revealed

In 1971, *The New York Times* found itself in possession of a publishing scoop. A top-secret study detailing the United States' political and military involvement in Vietnam from 1945 to 1967 was leaked to the paper by Daniel Ellsberg, a contributor to the document. The Pentagon Papers, as they were known, revealed how politicians and military leaders in previous U.S. governments had sometimes lied or covered up incidents during the war. Nixon tried to prevent their publication, but the Supreme Court allowed them to be published. Many Americans were shocked at the deceitful conduct of their government. Antiwar sentiment grew as a result and more demonstrators and protesters took to the streets.

Fierce fighting in Laos in 1971. The invasion of Laos was carried out by ARVN ground troops. It was intended to test the effectiveness of "Vietnamization."

bombing raids against North Vietnam, and shoring up support for the South Vietnamese government now led by Nguyen Van Thieu. By the end of 1972, South Vietnam had the world's fourth-largest air force, fourth-largest army, and fifth-largest navy.

The United States sought to tackle the Vietcong in two other ways. Operation Phoenix used the intelligence services and U.S. and ARVN special forces in an effort to identify and neutralize the political infrastructure that was directing and supporting the Vietcong in areas under South Vietnam's control. It was brutal and led to the deaths of an estimated 17,000 Vietnamese, but it was considered a success because it removed many Communist groups from South Vietnam. The United States also realized that it must try to undermine the Vietcong's tactic of building support in South Vietnamese villages. An effort was made to win over South Vietnamese "hearts and minds" through public

to allow the United States to withdraw all its troops. This time, a major operation to seek out Communist forces beyond Vietnam's borders and to attack the Ho Chi Minh Trail supply route was conducted in Laos. It was carried out solely by the ARVN but only achieved limited success.

Vietnamization also involved massive supplies of arms and training to South Vietnamese forces, stepping up the

ARVN soldiers surround the bodies of two North Vietnamese men killed in fighting during the Easter Offensive in 1972. A full-scale invasion of South Vietnam was prevented, but North Vietnam did gain large areas of South Vietnamese territory.

building projects such as bridges, roads, schools, and medical centers.

A SURPRISE ATTACK

It seemed at the end of 1971 that Vietnamization was working. The South Vietnamese were running all the combat operations on the ground even though they still needed air support from the United States. In a deliberate effort to test their strength, the North Vietnamese launched a surprise Easter Offensive on March 30, 1972. Around 130,000 North Vietnamese troops occupied Quang Tri province and attacked part of the Central Highlands and regions north of Saigon.

Helping the South Vietnamese help themselves

The goal for Nixon was an honorable exit from the war that would leave South Vietnam secure. He said:

"The nation's objective should be to help the South Vietnamese fight the war and not fight it for them. If they do not assume the majority of the burden in their own defense, they cannot be saved."

President Richard Nixon quoted in Stephen Ambrose, *Nixon: The Triumph of a Politician* (Simon & Schuster, 1989)

The tactics that the North Vietnamese adopted came as a surprise. Rather than continue with guerrilla operations, they chose to fight a conventional war, with large numbers of troops, supplies, and heavy weaponry committed to open battle. For this, the North Vietnamese needed bases and supply routes along which to transport fuel and ammunition. U.S. aircraft, equipped with the latest generation of smart weapons, found it quite easy to hit the large formations of North Vietnamese troops and their bases and supply routes from the air. A series of U.S. bombing raids, called Operation Linebacker, devastated their military lines, but nevertheless the North Vietnamese did make territorial gains in South Vietnam during the Easter Offensive.

PEACE TALKS IN PARIS

The shock of this offensive kickstarted the process of peace negotiation, which had been taking place off and on since 1969. Formal talks were held in Paris and were attended by representatives of all sides. Kissinger and Le Duc Tho, North Vietnam's chief negotiator, also held meetings in secret. In October 1972, a month before the U.S. presidential election, the prize seemed to be within reach. However, Thieu's South Vietnamese government rejected the deal, fearing that the United States was about to abandon the country to

North Vietnam's chief negotiator, Le Duc Tho (center right) and Secretary of State Henry Kissinger (left) agreed to cease-fire terms during the Paris Peace Talks in June 1973.

NVA prisoners are welcomed home by fellow North Vietnamese. The return of captured prisoners of war within sixty days was part of the peace agreement signed in 1973. The United States believed that some captured U.S. servicemen were not handed over and the issue remained a bone of contention.

the mercy of the Communists. Nixon was reelected in November and urged the North Vietnamese to reenter peace negotiations. He also warned the South Vietnamese government that he would make an agreement with or without their cooperation. When the negotiations stalled, Nixon ordered a huge bombing campaign against targets in North Vietnam to begin in December 1972. Operation Linebacker II saw the heaviest bomber strikes launched by the U.S. Air Force since the end of World War II. It destroyed many military targets and killed 1,600 civilians. It was halted in January 1973. A peace deal, the Paris Peace Accords, was finally agreed on a few days later.

The deal was intended to end direct U.S. military involvement in Vietnam and stop the fighting between North and South. It was signed on January 27, 1973. The United States agreed to withdraw all its combat troops from Vietnam within sixty days in exchange for the release of American prisoners of war. A cease-fire would be declared throughout Indochina. In March 1973, the North Vietnamese released 691 American prisoners, mostly captured aircrew. On March 29, the last U.S. ground troops left South Vietnam. Only military advisors and support staff remained behind.

NIXON RESIGNS

Although U.S. troops had departed, localized fighting dragged on in 1973. President Thieu was worried that, deprived of American protection and with parts of South Vietnam under NVA control, it was only a matter of time before the North Vietnamese would seek to take over more territory. Nixon

TURNING POINTS IN HISTORY

Would the U.S. respond?

Sensing their opportunity, the North Vietnamese were ready to invade South Vietnam at the end of 1974, but they held back for fear of drawing the United States back into the war. They decided to test U.S. resolve by making a strategic attack on a single South Vietnamese province, Phuoc Long, some 100 miles (160 km) north of Saigon. Two divisions of NVA soldiers, commanded by General Tran Van Tra, swept through the province in December 1974. ARVN resistance was overwhelmed and the province was captured within three weeks. Nixon's successor, President Gerald Ford, limited his response to diplomatic protests.

had given Thieu a written promise that the United States would continue to support South Vietnam and protect it from any future invasion by North Vietnam. However, in 1974, Nixon resigned from office, disgraced by the Watergate scandal. Congress passed a law that prevented a U.S. president from sending troops abroad without its explicit approval, and Congress at that time was strongly opposed to reentering the Vietnam conflict.

South Vietnam's economy, which was weak anyway, suffered a massive blow in 1974. The U.S. military aid budget to the country was slashed in half. It dropped to $1.1 billion, less than half the 1973 figure. The ARVN found itself crippled by a lack of money. Fuel, spare parts, and ammunition ran low, and the morale of troops suffered. Many

ARVN mechanized troops on patrol in South Vietnam. When U.S. financial aid was slashed, the South Vietnamese government struggled to finance its forces, since the ARVN cost almost $3 billion a year to run. The South Vietnamese army soon ran short of supplies and fuel.

The gates of the Presidential Palace in Saigon are smashed to the ground by an NVA tank on April 30, 1975. The capture of the palace in the heart of South Vietnam's capital city marked the end of the war for South Vietnam. The two Vietnams were formally reunited the following year.

soldiers could not even afford to feed their families. North Vietnam was in a much stronger position, and by the end of 1974 it was ready to launch a decisive attack. The first target was Phuoc Long province, and the success of this action gave the green light for a general offensive in South Vietnam. This began in March 1975 and advances were rapid. The city of Hue was captured on March 26 and Da Nang, south of Hue, fell three days later.

SURRENDER OF THE SOUTH

Anxious to defend the capital Saigon, Thieu ordered his troops to retreat from the Central Highlands southward so that they could regroup. It was a bad mistake. The few routes south from the Central Highlands became jammed with convoys of troops and fleeing civilians who came under heavy attack from

NVA artillery. It is estimated that over 100,000 people died or were captured in the chaos. The remaining ARVN in the north of South Vietnam were cut off and quickly defeated. NVA troops pressed on remorselessly and were soon on the outskirts of Saigon. An atmosphere of panic gripped the South Vietnamese.

Thieu resigned on April 21, and his parting words included a fierce denunciation of the United States. The North Vietnamese knew that victory was in their grasp and began the final assault on Saigon. A last-minute evacuation was organized by the remaining U.S. personnel in the country and an estimated 50,000 people were airlifted out of Saigon before NVA tanks crashed through the gates of the Presidential Palace. The South Vietnamese government formally surrendered on April 30, 1975. In

Broken promises

South Vietnamese leader Thieu was bitterly critical of the Americans for not honoring their promises. During a radio and TV broadcast to announce his resignation, he said:

"At the time of the peace agreement the United States agreed to replace equipment on a one-by-one basis. . . . But the United States did not keep its word. Is an American's word reliable these days? The United States did not keep its promise to help us fight for freedom and it was in the same fight that the United States lost 50,000 of its young men."

BBC TV archive

1976, the two halves of Vietnam were reunified and the country was renamed the Socialist Republic of Vietnam; Saigon became Ho Chi Minh City.

A Shattered Country

The nation was reunified, but physically Vietnam was in ruins. The casualty list ran to as many as 5 million dead and hundreds of thousands wounded. An estimated 879,000 of the population in 1975 were orphans. Factories, schools, hospitals, transport infrastructure, and sanitation systems were smashed. Chemical defoliants and mines had ruined much of the farmland, and famines and food shortages would

One of the most controversial aspects of the U.S. presence in Southeast Asia was the use of chemical defoliants such as Agent Orange to destroy jungle cover concealing the Vietcong forces and to damage their crops.

plague Vietnam for the next fifteen years. There was another deadly legacy: chemicals present in one commonly used defoliant, Agent Orange, were later proved to cause cancer.

The new regime that ruled South Vietnam cracked down harshly on old enemies. About 60,000 South Vietnamese government and army members and supporters of the war against Communism were executed, and thousands more were sent to prison camps. Around a million people were forcibly resettled, mostly being relocated from South Vietnam's cities into the countryside. Some minority groups were persecuted, particularly the Chinese in Vietnam, many of whom were relatively wealthy. Their money was confiscated and Chinese newspapers

and schools were shut down. Despite the assistance China had given to North Vietnam during the early part of the war, relations between the two countries had grown sour. In 1979, China even staged a limited invasion of Vietnam.

It is believed that around 1.5 million Vietnamese "boat people" fled the country in the late 1970s by stowing away on foreign ships or setting sail in flimsy boats and rafts. They were trying to escape from their feared Communist masters. Many perished en route, while thousands more arrived as penniless refugees in other countries in Southeast Asia.

Exact casualty figures are not available, but estimates suggest that as a result of the war, between 150,000 and 225,000 members of the South Vietnamese army were killed, and as many as double that number were severely injured. Upward of 1.1 million North Vietnamese and Vietcong were

WHY DID IT HAPPEN

Who was at fault?

The failure of South Vietnam to defeat the North prompts the question: were the South Vietnamese abandoned to their fate by the United States, or did they fail to defend themselves adequately despite being well supplied with U.S. money and armaments? Nixon maintained that "In early 1973, when we left South Vietnam, we left it in a strong position militarily. . . . We had tried to tip the balance of power toward the South Vietnamese by launching a massive resupply effort in late 1972."

Others argue that South Vietnam could not afford to operate the complex and expensive U.S. equipment, and point out that South Vietnam was undermined by massive cuts in aid and that America was prepared to negotiate politically with North Vietnam. Historian Ian Beckett observes, "Nixon's only real aim was to withdraw US troops with honour, and little was done to ensure the future security of South Vietnam."

Richard Nixon, *No More Vietnams* (Arbor House Publishing, 1987); Ian Beckett, *Southeast Asia From 1945* (Franklin Watts, 1986)

Faced with Communist rule, many Vietnamese chose to flee their country by boat. These refugees reached Hong Kong after a dangerous journey across the South China Sea in 1979.

dead and 600,000 wounded. In addition, over 1 million Vietnamese civilians were killed. The Americans lost 47,000 personnel killed in combat and 11,000 more from other causes such as disease. U.S. allies also suffered casualties: South Korea lost 4,500, Australia more than 500, and Thailand 350.

An Enduring Legacy

The Vietnam War and its aftermath cast a long shadow over American politics for many years. The war had cost the United States over $120 billion and had deeply divided public opinion. The country's image as a military and political superpower had also been damaged by the conflict.

American foreign policy became more cautious—the country did not commit large numbers of troops to any conflict overseas for almost two decades, until the 1991 Gulf War against Iraq. Issues surrounding the war continued to stir up public debate in the United States. Many families campaigned to learn the fate of American personnel labeled as missing in action (MIA). The treatment that returning Vietnam veterans received from their own countrymen also caused controversy. Some 3 million Americans had served during the Vietnam War, and many thousands of them found it extremely hard to reintegrate into normal life.

President Ronald Reagan and his wife, Nancy, at the Vietnam Veterans Memorial Wall in Washington, D.C. The wall is carved with the names of more than 58,000 Americans who lost their lives in the war.

VIETNAM TIMELINE

1941 Viet Minh formed with the aim of fighting for Vietnam's independence

1945 Ho Chi Minh declares Vietnam independent of French rule and creates a provisional government

1949 Communists under Mao Zedong take control of China

1954 May: Viet Minh defeat French at Dien Bien Phu. French rule in Vietnam ends

July: The agreements reached at the Geneva Conference mean that Vietnam is temporarily divided into two parts.

1955 October: Bao Dai deposed from power in South Vietnam, replaced by Ngo Dinh Diem as South Vietnam's first president

1959 Construction of the Ho Chi Minh Trail starts. Guerrilla warfare supported by North Vietnam breaks out in South Vietnam

1961 U.S. president John F. Kennedy announces increased military aid to South Vietnam

1963 January: Vietcong units defeat South Vietnamese Army (ARVN) in Battle of Ap Bac

November 1–2: President Diem of South Vietnam assassinated

November 22: Kennedy assassinated and succeeded by Lyndon Johnson

1964 August: Gulf of Tonkin incident leads to a major escalation of U.S. forces in Vietnam

1965 February: Heavy bombing campaign against North Vietnam—Operation Rolling Thunder—begins

1967 October: Major antiwar protests in the United States begin in Washington, D.C., and elsewhere

1968 January–February: Tet Offensive: North Vietnamese and Vietcong forces attack South Vietnamese cities

March: My Lai massacre of civilians by U.S. forces. News of the massacre breaks the following year, causing public outrage

November: Richard Nixon succeeds Lyndon Johnson as U.S. president

1969 April: U.S. troop levels in Vietnam peak at over 540,000

June: President Nixon announces policy of Vietnamization; limited troop withdrawals begin

1972 April: Launch of Easter Offensive by the North Vietnamese Army

May: Quang Tri City falls to the North Vietnamese

December: Operation Linebacker II: bombing of North Vietnam by U.S.

1973 January 27: Paris peace agreement signed by the United States and North Vietnam

1974 August: Nixon resigns and is succeeded as president by Gerald Ford.

December: North Vietnam launches offensive on Phuoc Long province

1975 April 30: South Vietnam's capital Saigon falls to North Vietnamese troops. South Vietnam surrenders

1976 Vietnam becomes one country, the Socialist Republic of Vietnam, and Saigon is renamed Ho Chi Minh City

GLOSSARY

ARVN Army of the Republic of Vietnam, the South Vietnamese military forces on the ground.

Cold War Distrustful and hostile relationship between the Soviet Union and its allies and the United States and its allies that developed shortly after World War II.

Communist Someone who believes in Communism, a political system in which the state's property and wealth is owned by the people.

conventional warfare The use of regular armed forces fighting battles in the open with heavy arms and equipment.

coup The overthrow of a government by a small group, often members of the army.

covert Performed in secret.

defoliant A chemical that kills the leaves of trees and plants.

dictatorship A country run by a single person, a dictator, who has absolute power.

domino theory The notion that if one country in a region were to fall to Communism, then other countries would quickly fall to Communism as well.

guerrillas Soldiers, not part of a regular army, who use surprise attacks and stay hidden in order to combat an army with greater numbers or superior weaponry.

infiltrate To enter a group or region secretly.

intelligence Information important to a country or group's security, often concerning enemy weapons and troop movements.

NLF National Liberation Front, an organization established in 1960 dedicated to overthrowing the South Vietnamese government. The military arm of the NLF was known as the Vietcong.

NVA The North Vietnamese Army, also referred to in some texts as the People's Army of North Vietnam, or PAVN.

propaganda Deliberate methods of communication and influence used to persuade people to believe certain ideas or to behave in a certain way.

reunification The act of bringing a divided country together into one nation.

Vietcong Term used to describe the communist guerrilla fighters operating in South Vietnam.

FURTHER INFORMATION

Books:
Canwell, Diane. *African Americans in the Vietnam War*. New York: World Almanac, 2005.
Dunn, John M. *A History of U.S. Involvement*. San Diego: Lucent Books, 2001.
Gavin, Philip. *The Fall of Vietnam*. San Diego: Lucent Books, 2003.
Levy, Debbie. *The Vietnam War*. Minneapolis, MN: Lerner, 2004.

Web Sites:
Battlefield Vietnam
(www.pbs.org/battlefieldvietnam)
The Vietnam Center and Archive
(www.vietnam.ttu.edu/index.htm)
Vietnam Online
(www.pbs.org/wgbh/amex/vietnam/index.html)
The Vietnam Veterans Memorial Wall Page
(thewall-usa.com)

INDEX

Numbers in **bold** refer to pictures